Pitter and Patter

by Martha Sullivan

Illustrated by Cathy Morrison

Dawn Publications

To Dad, who always saw the beauty in nature. — MS

To Mason & Makenzie Sandoval, no matter where life takes you,
you'll always find home with each other. — CM

Back matter contributed by Carol L. Malnor and Martha Sullivan

Library of Congress Cataloging-in-Publication Data

Sullivan, Martha, author.
Pitter and Patter / by Martha Sullivan ; illustrated by Cathy Morrison. -- First edition.
pages cm
Summary: "The water cycle becomes a down-to-earth reality when children follow Pitter on his overland journey from cloud to ocean, and Patter on her journey from cloud to ocean by way of an underground route. In the ocean they meet and join in a cloud once again. 'Explore More' endnotes provide additional explanations of water cycle principles"-- Provided by the publisher.
Audience: Ages 4-10.
Audience: K to grade 4.
ISBN 978-1-58469-508-0 (hardback) -- ISBN 978-1-58469-509-7 (pbk.) 1. Hydrologic cycle--Juvenile literature. 2. Water--Juvenile literature. I. Morrison, Cathy, illustrator. II. Title.

GB848.S85 2015
551.48--dc23

2014031420

Book design and computer production by Patty Arnold, *Menagerie Design & Publishing*
Manufactured by Regent Publishing Services, Hong Kong
Printed December, 2014, in ShenZhen, Guangdong, China

10 9 8 7 6 5 4 3 2 1

First Edition

DAWN PUBLICATIONS
12402 Bitney Springs Road
Nevada City, CA 95959
530-274-7775
nature@dawnpub.com

Pitter and Patter dropped from
a cool, gray cloud one day.

Pitter landed on the leaf
of an oak tree.
Hello, squirrel.
Good morning, blue jay.
Rise and shine, caterpillar.

He dripped into the stream below.
Hello, crayfish.
Howdy, snake.
Best wishes for the day, mayfly.

The stream carried Pitter down into the valley.

Hello, fox.

Greetings, deer.

A pleasure to see you again, hawk.

It flowed into a winding river.
Hello, trout.
Good day, dragonfly.
All good things to you, otter.

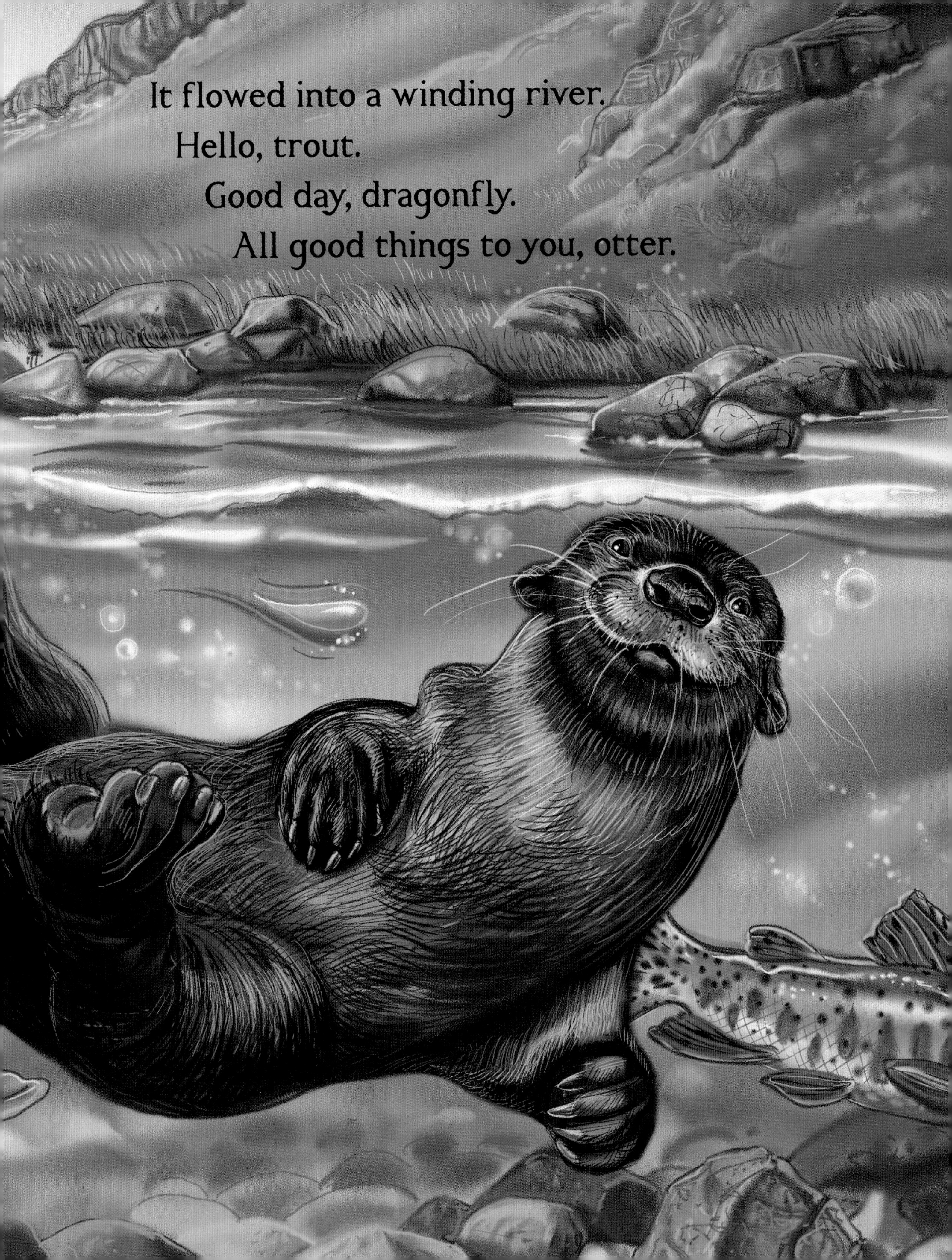

The river poured into a wetland of tall, swaying grasses.

Hello, crab.

So nice to meet you, shrimp.

A happy day to you, heron.

The wetlands met the ocean.
Hello, turtle.
A pleasure as always, ray.
See you again soon, jellyfish.

Meanwhile, Patter had landed
in a spring meadow.
Hello, daisy.
Good morning, bee.
Rise and shine, butterfly.

She trickled down into the
dark, damp soil.
HELLOOOOW! ~ Is anybody here?

Oh hi there, ant.
Howdy, earthworm.
Best wishes for the day, mole.

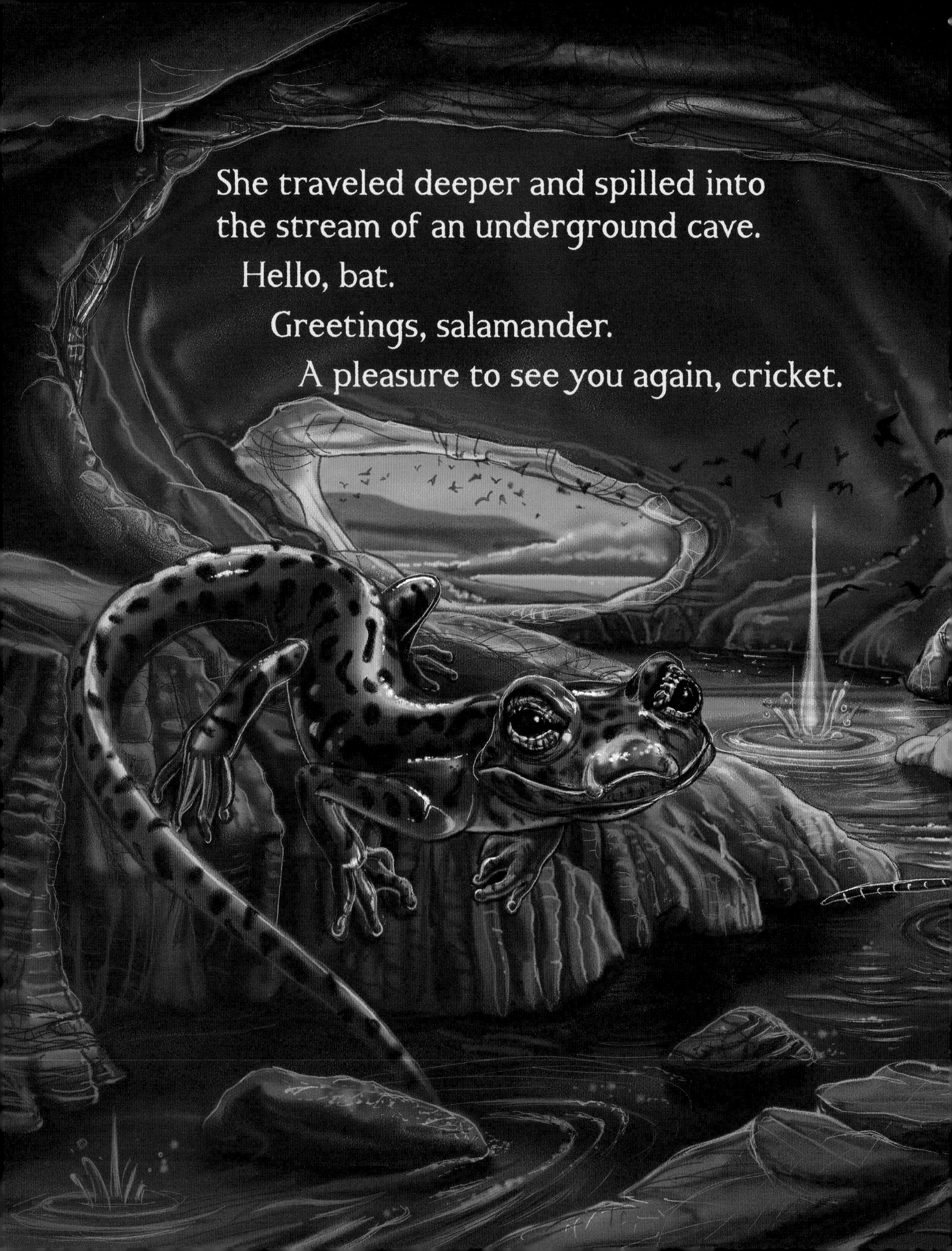

She traveled deeper and spilled into
the stream of an underground cave.

Hello, bat.

Greetings, salamander.

A pleasure to see you again, cricket.

The stream flowed into a river.
Hello, beaver.
Good day, mink.
All good things to you, salmon.

And the river swept Patter out to sea.
A happy day to you, seal.
So nice to meet you, squid.
Hello, PITTER!

In a mist of sea spray, Pitter and Patter
met the warm rays of the sun.
They became warmer and warmer.
They became lighter and lighter.
They floated up into the sky.

Where they joined their old friend,
the gray cloud.

STATES OF MATTER
Same but Different

Water in a puddle is **liquid**. When the sun dries it, the water becomes water vapor—a **gas**. When it gets cold and a puddle freezes, the water becomes ice, a **solid**.

THE WATER CYCLE
Around and Around

Water is constantly changing and moving. It forms clouds, falls to the earth, and returns to the clouds again. It's the same water, and it's reused over and over again. It's the same water that rained down on dinosaurs! Water's journey is called **the water cycle**.

1. **Evaporation**: Water is warmed and becomes water **vapor**. Can you see the word vapor hidden in the word evaporate?
2. **Condensation**: Water vapor cools as it rises and becomes a cloud of water droplets. Clouds are made of billions of water droplets.
3. **Precipitation**: Water droplets stick together until they get so big and heavy that they fall as rain, snow, hail, or sleet.

THE WATERSHED
Going Down!

When water falls from the sky and lands on the ground, it begins its journey downhill. The journey might take it from small streams to large rivers to enormous oceans. Sometimes the journey even happens underground. The area of land that collects water and drains it into large body of water, like a lake or ocean, is called a **watershed**.

Gray Cloud
Water vapor becomes water drops
CONDENSATION
Follow Pitter
Water falls from clouds
PRECIPITATION
Oak Tree
Water changes to water vapor
and rises
EVAPORATION
Stream
Valley
Water gathers in many places
COLLECTION
River
Wetland
Ocean

Same but Different – STATES OF MATTER

Water is matter and exists in three states: solid, liquid, or gas. Water changes its state depending on the amount of energy (heat) that is available. As the temperature increases, the amount of energy increases, and water molecules move faster.

Solid Water—*ice, snow,* or *hail.* Water becomes solid when the temperature is at or below freezing. Freezing temperatures mean that there is little energy available to the water molecules. They huddle close together in a fixed position. Solid water, such as an ice cube, retains its shape.

Liquid Water—just called *water.* When the temperature increases to above freezing, water molecules are able to move around more because there is more energy available to them. However, they still remain close to one another. Liquid water, like a river, flows.

Gas Water—water *vapor.* When water is heated, giving it more energy, the molecules spread out and lose contact with one another and water becomes a gas. In other words, liquid water has *evaporated* and become water vapor.

Demonstration: Changing States

Put several ice cubes in a saucepan. Put the pan on a hot plate and turn up the heat. Have students watch the ice melt. Explain that heat changed the "state" of the water from solid to liquid. Use a ruler to measure the amount of water in the pan. Then boil the water for two minutes and measure it again. Ask children where the water went. Did they see it? Explain that heat changed the water from a liquid to a gas, called water vapor. Evaporating water is usually invisible to the eye, but may sometimes be seen as steam.

Around and Around – THE WATER CYCLE

There is a constant amount of water on Earth. The water that falls to the ground from clouds is not new to the planet. The water that flows through each of us every day is the same water that, over the course of billions of years, has flowed through birds, bees, mushrooms, and trees. Water is recycled through the processes of *precipitation, evaporation,* and *condensation.* Precipitation falls from clouds to the earth's surface, evaporates, and condenses into clouds again. This cycle repeats again and again.

Activity: Dramatic Play

Act out the water cycle using puppets and props. Begin by having small groups of children make puppets of Pitter or Patter, the sun, and the gray cloud. Then create a simple set of places from the story using everyday items: towels for streams and rivers, a pile of pillows for a wetland or ocean, and a blanket over a chair as a cave. If playing outside, the top of an outdoor play structure could serve as the top of an oak tree, a slide as a river, and a low area as the ocean. Have a group of children use their puppets to narrate either Pitter's or Patter's journey as the children physically move through the landscape set. Ask them to use the words *precipitation, evaporation, condensation* when Pitter and Patter fall as rain, are warmed by the sun, and condense in the gray cloud. The various animals Pitter and Patter meet along the way may be enacted by children or with additional puppets.

Going Down – THE WATERSHED

Pitter and Patter travel through a watershed—a basin of land that collects water into a single body of water. Although they drop in different places and take notably different paths, they both end up in the same ocean at the end of their respective journeys. But is it really the end? No, the water cycle is endless.

Activity: Sand Table Watershed

It can be difficult for children to envision a watershed because it is so large. Using a sand table allows children to see an entire watershed in a smaller scale. Fill your sand table with sand and/or soil. Have children sculpt the landscape based on the story, including hillsides, valleys and waterways. Place toy trees and animals throughout the scene. Tilt the table slightly downward at one end and suspend a hose with a spray nozzle over the table to simulate rain. Have children watch how the water moves through the watershed they have created. Emphasize that liquid water always flows downward. Explain that everyone lives in a watershed. Ask them to think about how their activities might affect their watershed. Demonstrate this concept by dropping small bits of trash on the sand table and seeing where the trash ends up when the water flows. Using a simple map, show children the watershed where they live.

Around and Through – WATER IN HABITATS AND HUMANS

Following Pitter and Patter through the watershed illustrates the way water connects various habitats and the plants and animals that live in them. All living organisms require water. It is the medium for the chemical reactions that sustain life. In plants, water is taken in by the roots carrying with it important minerals that plants need. This mineral-rich water travels up through the plant eventually reaching the leaves where it evaporates into the surrounding air in a process known as transpiration. In animals, water is an important transport medium, too, carrying nutrients and removing waste. Water also helps animals maintain their correct body temperature, even when the environment gets very hot or cold. To accomplish all of these tasks, plants and animals take in water and release it back into the environment. This flow of water through living things is another aspect of the water cycle.

Activity: Watershed Habitats

Refer to the illustrations in the book and identify the habitats that Pitter and Patter flow through: temperate forest (woodland), fresh water (stream, river, and wetland), grassland (meadow), and salt water (ocean). Ask children to identify the plants and animals in each habitat. Explain that all living things depend on water and lead a discussion about how animals in the story depend upon water.

Activity: Wonderful Water

With your children, brainstorm a list of all the ways they use water. Possible responses include using water for bathing, cleaning, cooking, flushing, cooling, drinking, and watering. Also remind children that water is fun! They can run through it, splash in it, swim in it, float on it, spray it, follow it, race sticks on it, and skip stones upon it. Have children create a "Wonderful Water" bulletin board by making drawings of the activities from the list. Include a brief explanation for each drawing. You may use this activity as a springboard for introducing the topic of water conservation, helping children understand that the way they use water makes a difference because their actions affect the entire water cycle.

Educators: Dawn Publications offers another popular book about the water cycle for somewhat older children, *A Drop Around the World.* Additionally, *A Teacher's Guide to A Drop Around the World* is available as an ebook. There are many wonderful resources online, including activities and lesson plans. Scan this code to go directly to additional activities and lesson plans for *Pitter and Patter*, or go to www.dawnpub.com and click on "Activities" for this and other books.

Martha Sullivan is a children's book author with a special interest in nature and sustainability. Born and raised in the US, Martha has also lived in Belgium, Austria, the UK, and most recently, County Clare, Ireland, where she enjoys kayaking, hiking, set-dancing, and gardening. Martha is passionate about her mission—helping children to connect with the natural world so that they are primed to protect it later in life. A Master's thesis on Education for Sustainable Development through the University of Bath was the catalyst that moved Martha from the classroom where she taught Biology for fifteen years to the writer's desk. She now focuses on stories that help children to understand the importance of biodiversity and conservation.

Cathy Morrison is an award-winning illustrator who lives in Colorado, within view of both the Great Plains and the Rocky Mountains. She watches the plants, the animals, and rain—all close up and personal. She began her career in animation and graphic design, but discovered her passion for children's book illustration while raising her two children. After several years illustrating with traditional media, she now works digitally, which helps the publisher adapt the art into interactive book apps. This is Cathy's second book for Dawn Publications.

Other Books, E-books, and Interactive Book Apps

Pitter and Patter — This book is also available as a playful interactive app in which children can follow Pitter and Patter's journeys, identify the creatures that they encounter, and make their way around the water cycle and through the watershed.

To teach the water cycle to older children (7-10) we recommend *A Drop Around the World*.

The Prairie that Nature Built — This book also has an app, in which the diggers dig, the birds, fly, and the grazers munch—and much more — when you touch them.

The Mouse and the Meadow — Experience the vibrant and sometimes dangerous nature of meadow life from a mouse's eye-view. **In the app**, touch the characters and see them move! *This book also has a free Pop-Up App.*

The Swamp Where Gator Hides — Look for gator hiding in the algae, and learn about the turtle, vole, bobcat, duck, sunfish, and other animals that are home there. **In the app**, help them escape gator's fast-approaching jaws!

Noisy Bug Sing-Along — An amazing concert of sounds is happening every day, made by insects that have no vocal chords! **In the app**, see how they move different body parts to make sounds, then play the matching game.

Noisy Frog Sing-Along — See the many kinds of frogs that make all kinds of sounds–without ever opening their mouths! **In the app**, watch their bulgy throat pouches expand, then play the game by matching their sounds (and sound waves) with each kind of frog.

Over in the Ocean — Coral reefs are teeming with colorful mamas and babies. You can count and sing along. **In the app**, little fingers can make the octopus squirt, and the pufferfish puff! Then play the counting game challenge to find all 55 babies hiding in the coral reef.

Over in the Jungle — Count, clap, and sing among enchanting rainforest animals and their babies. **In the app**, watch the ocelots pounce, parrots squawk, and boas squeeze – and then find all the babies hiding in the jungle floor and canopy.

Dawn Publications is dedicated to inspiring in children a deeper understanding and appreciation for all life on Earth. You can browse through our titles, download resources for teachers, and order at www.dawnpub.com or call 800-545-7475.